TIWI GIRL

Tiwi Girl first published in 2015 by the Indigenous Literacy Foundation
Nginingawila Ngirramini: Our Story first published in 2015 by Hachette Australia (an imprint of Hachette Australia Pty Ltd)
This edition published in 2026 by the Indigenous Literacy Foundation

Gadigal Country
Level 17/207 Kent Street
Sydney NSW 2000
ilf.org.au

Cataloguing-in-Publication details are available from the National Library of Australia

www.trove.nla.gov.au

ISBN 9781923456914

Cover and internal illustrations by Rusinya Brooks
Design, map and typesetting by Steven Dunbar
Printed and bound in Australia by McPherson's Printing Group

TIWI GIRL

and other stories

Tiwi College Alalinguwi Jarrakarlinga

INDIGENOUS
LITERACY
FOUNDATION™

contents

FOREWORD

by Shelley Ware

As an ambassador of the Indigenous Literacy Foundation (ILF), I have had the joy and privilege of working on the *Create Initiative* program with students from Tiwi College for many years now, mentoring them along with ambassadors Alison Lester and David Lawrence and Tictac Moore, formerly an assistant teacher at Tiwi College but who now works for the ILF.

Through my work with the ILF, and connection to this beautiful community, I have got to know these authors, who are now strong pillars of the Tiwi Community. They are leaders, educators, artists, workers, change makers and mothers, who continue to be an inspiration to their Community.

Tiwi Girl shares truths of what life as a typical teenager on Tiwi looks like, and it's also a story that teenagers around the world can see themselves in. *Tiwi Girl* allows young people, educators and parents to have open and honest conversations with their teenager/s about how, together, they can navigate adolescence.

Every time I visit, the authors of *Tiwi Girl*, as well as their families and wider Community!, always ask me, "Where is Alison Lester?" and "When is she coming back?". Alison is loved in Tiwi because she she has visited and done many workshops at Tiwi College and Milikapiti, and the connections made in this time are still felt today.

In this special new edition of *Tiwi Girl*, we see the inclusion of *Nginingawila Ngirramini: Our Story*, written during Create the following year and authored mostly by the same students, with ILF Ambassador Dr Anita Heiss and author Pamela Freeman.

Nginingawila Ngirramini: Our Story shares the young Tiwi girls' hopes, dreams, aspirations, lived experiences, and who inspires them to be the best version of themselves. A collection of letters to heroes, stories shared of their sacred places and the happiest moments of their lives. Together this new edition is titled *Tiwi Girl and Other Stories*.

The impact of *Tiwi Girl and Other Stories* goes

beyond the Tiwi Islands and carries a legacy I know the authors of this incredible book are proud of – today and beyond – as a gift for the next generations. Enjoy reading *Tiwi Girl and Other Stories* and hopefully, one day, you will make it to Tiwi, where you can enjoy their Country and the people who are full of wisdom, generosity and love for everyone.

Shelley Ware
ILF Ambassador

ABOUT THIS BOOK

This new edition of *Tiwi Girl* combines works produced during two of the Indigenous Literacy Foundation's *Create Initiatives*. This initiative for young women partners with publishers, and is facilitated by author and illustrator mentors, to create stories, cultivate knowledge and grow self-esteem.

The *Tiwi Girl* story was written in September 2024, when nine young women, all senior students at Tiwi College, travelled to Sydney with their teachers. The host publisher, HarperCollins, shared its publishing expertise and provided a wonderful space to work in. Indigenous Literacy Foundation Lifetime Ambassador and mentor, Alison Lester, guided the young women through brainstorming, story mapping and writing sessions, and then helped them to illustrate the story.

The students wrote collaboratively, creating a

fictional story they all wanted to tell and share. Tiwi College, the Tiwi Islands and Tiwi life were the inspiration behind *Tiwi Girl*. On their return home, the young women continued to work on the story with fellow students in the Senior Girls class.

In 2015, the girls returned to Sydney, this time hosted by Hachette Australia and with Indigenous Literacy Foundation Lifetime Ambassador Dr Anita Heiss as mentor, assisted by author Pamela Freeman. In this workshop they developed individual pieces, non-fiction stories about their heroes, their sacred places and the happiest and proudest moments of their lives.

The result was *Nginingawila Ngirramini* – Tiwi for 'Our Story' – a book that is a celebration of pride and a window into the lives of nine talented, intelligent and funny girls from the Tiwi Islands.

In her original introduction, Dr Heiss said that the book, "celebrates the diverse voices of nine talented and motivated young women, who have enthusiastically engaged with the gruelling process of writing to deadlines, while being true to their own creativity. Whether writing about their Elders, family, music or sporting legends as their heroes, the authors within have demonstrated respect and gratitude for those who have impacted most on their lives through work and leadership."

Both the *Tiwi Girl* book and *Nginingawila Ngirramini: Our Story* were first published in 2015. This new combined volume seeks to bring the stories, both fiction and nonfiction, to a fresh audience.

TIWI GIRL

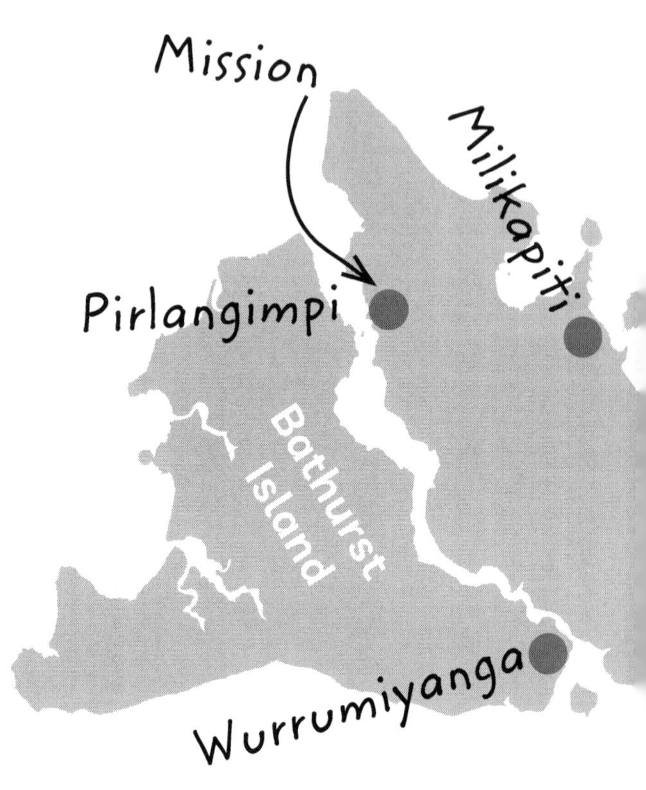

TIWI ISLANDS

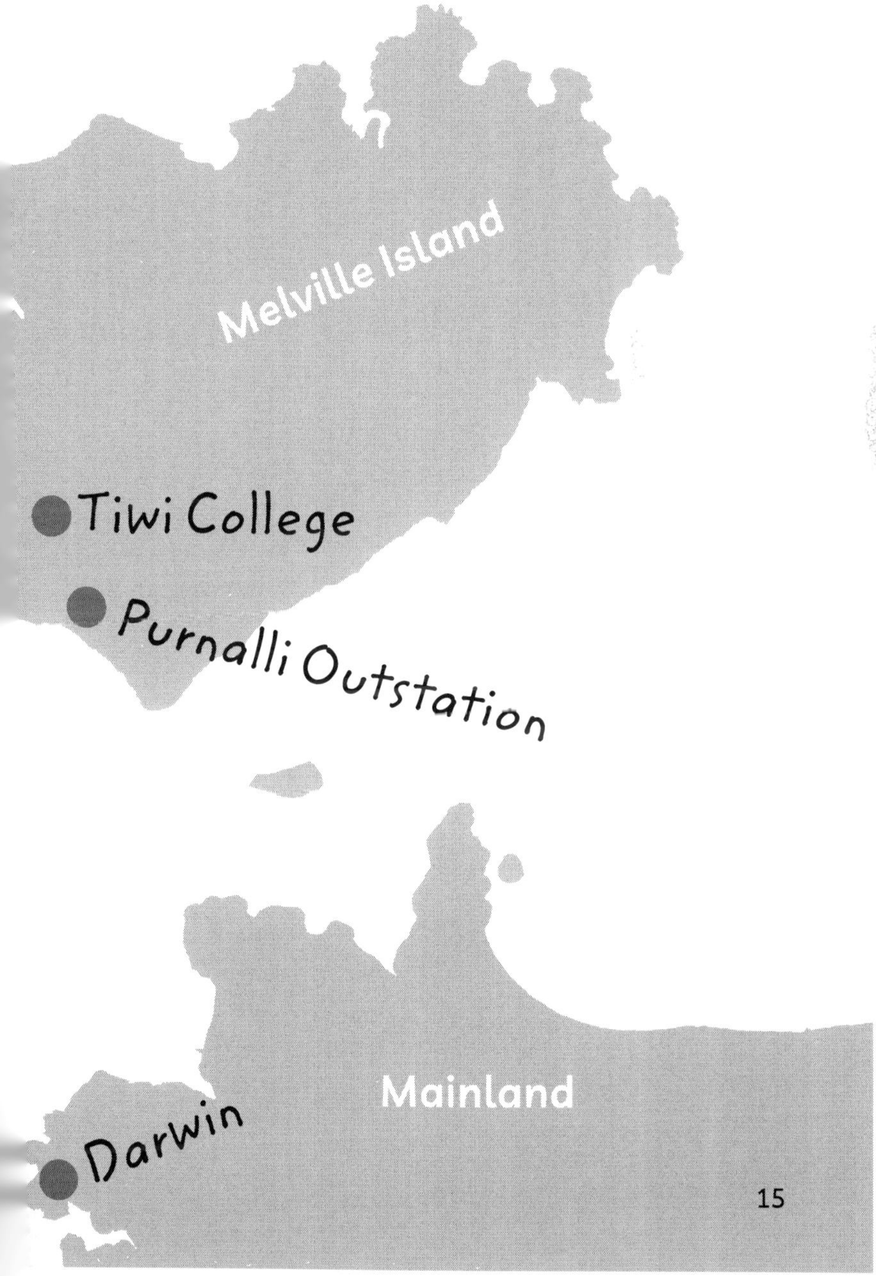

Melville Island

Tiwi College

Purnalli Outstation

Mainland

Darwin

1.

MIA lives at Purnalli outstation with her nanna, Maningawu Joy, and her twin brother Jake, cousin Gloria and baby niece Glorianna.

Maningawu has an upstairs house near the edge of a rocky cliff. A path leads down from the house to a beach with white sand, lush green mangroves and beautiful see-through water.

It's a very old house with three bedrooms and a big lounge area. Sometimes Mia and Maningawu sleep out in the lounge room because it's cooler there.

The house and all the furniture in it are made out of wood. There are no bookshelves and no pictures in frames. Photos are just stuck straight onto the walls.

When you walk into the house it smells really nice, like the flowers in the bush. Outside there are green triangular-shaped leaves everywhere you look and flowers as soft as jelly beans.

Mia and her family collect water in rainwater tanks, or they pump water to the house from the creek. The generator works well, but they need to make sure they've got a lot of petrol to keep it going.

They often sit around a fire outside to keep warm on cold nights. They love cooking bush tucker on the fire. The smell of it all roasting away makes their bellies rumble.

The house is a long way from any community and it's a very peaceful place to live. When Mia walks up the hill to get phone reception she always carries Glorianna on her back.

In the dry season, when everything goes brown, the rangers start burning off. You know it's the dry season because people's skin goes dry too and everyone starts using cream or baby oil on their arms and legs.

Mia loves the dry season: the weather is nice

and cold and there's no rain. It's the best time to go camping.

In the wet season it's very hot and everyone gets tired and sweaty. All the grass and trees come back to life, like everything is reborn. Before the first rain everything around you is black, then green shoots start to come through.

On weekends Mia and Jake like to go hunting. It's a good thing their grandpa, Aminayi John, left them his gun when he died. They're both good shots with the gun, but Mia is more accurate.

Mia and Jake almost always go out shooting for wallaby and buffalo to make sure there's enough meat to feed everyone. If Mia shoots a wallaby, Jake has to carry it home over his shoulders because he's stronger. If they shoot a buffalo, they get a car to take it home.

If they're not hunting for wallaby and buffalo, they spear barra or salmon at the beach for the family. Mia and Jake also love hunting in the mangroves for mud crabs, mud mussels, mangrove worms and long bums, which look like Snow Cones.

Maningawu is too old to walk through the thin

trees and pointy sticks in the bush, so Mia and Jake go hunting for her. They never come home empty-handed because they know Maningawu loves her bush tucker. She needs to eat food from the sea and bush to stay strong and healthy.

At the outstation they have their own veggie and fruit garden, so they don't have to go to the community all the time for fresh food—just on pay weeks, every fortnight.

Maningawu is on basic card. Every pay week half her pension goes into her basic card, and she uses that when she goes to the shop. It's good Maningawu is on basic card: that way people can't ask her for her leftover money to buy smokes and beer and other things.

Mia doesn't like going to the community because it's like a circus. She finds it too noisy. But sometimes she has to help with shopping or go to the clinic. Sometimes she goes there for football with the school team.

Mia doesn't like it when people are fighting, and she doesn't like seeing all the people gambling. Everyone gambles, even the kids.

2.

MIA and Jake get picked up in a troopy at the start of every week to go to boarding school. This is the closest high school to them. It's far away, so they stay all week. The road is usually dry and dusty with corrugations and potholes everywhere, so the driver has to be very careful.

In the wet season the road gets slippery and boggy. The school has to check cyclone watches in the wet season and sometimes the pick-ups are late.

When the driver goes around the community picking up the other kids it can be stressful, because some of them make excuses not to go to school. It can sometimes be a long waiting game until everyone is in the troopy.

On the way to school Mia sits by herself at the back, staring out the window, watching the trees and hearing the breeze rush by her ears.

One day they saw a dead buffalo on the side of the road. There were flies buzzing around and it stunk up the troopy so bad.

At boarding school, Mia lives in a family group home with ten other girls. Each morning she makes her bed, packs her lunch and gets ready for school. Each night she does her homework.

There's footy training two days a week. You have to train hard to get into the team. Mia is a good footballer, but she isn't a good listener. Maningawu is always asking if Mia is listening or if her ears are for decoration.

Mia loves singing and she sings everywhere, all day. Mia and the other girls also love hearing stories from their houseparents, mainly because they're from Fiji and have a different accent. Sometimes they say things funny, and Mia and all the girls giggle.

The girls are going away to a footy competition

and Mia wants to go with them, but sometimes she misses training.

Jake is a superstar. He bolts through everyone on the field. Mia can too, but Jake gets all the attention. Everyone says he plays like Cyril Rioli.

Mia starts to hang around with a group of girls who smoke cigarettes and start fights. She gets growled for not following the school rules. If Maningawu knew that Mia was following the wrong kids, she wouldn't be happy with Mia's new attitude.

One morning at Purnalli, a kookaburra swoops down onto the verandah at home and lands on the table where Maningawu is having her cup of tea. Maningawu knows right away that it's a sign something is wrong with Mia.

Later a car appears in the distance, and it looks like the school troopy. Sure enough, out jumps Mia. She's been suspended from school.

Mia gets a big growling from Maningawu, but later they sit around the fire talking about different choices. Maningawu tells Mia that she wasn't perfect when she was Mia's age but she thinks Mia is smart enough to make the right choices.

It's a beautiful night in the bush.

Maningawu tells Mia how she was stolen from her family when she was a little girl and taken to the mission at Garden Point. She was one of the Stolen Generations.

Maningawu's mum and dad lived at Menindee, thousands of kilometres away, somewhere in New South Wales. Little Joy was very homesick and wanted to run away from the mission, but she couldn't because the trackers always found the runaway kids and took them back.

At the mission things were tough, and it was hard for the kids to understand why they'd been taken away from their homes. They were treated like slaves and had to deal with racism every day.

When Maningawu was old enough, she moved out of the mission and became an assistant teacher at the local school. She fell in love with a boy named John who was a gardener at the school, and they got married and had a family.

The house Mia lives in above the beach is the house that Maningawu and Aminayi lived in all their married life. Aminayi planted their veggie and fruit garden out the back.

Aminayi was a tall and fit old man. He loved his hunting, but he also loved drinking and smoking. He was on dialysis and needed to go to the hospital at Wurrimiyanga on Bathurst Island, but he didn't want to travel. He died and they buried him near his house, under a mango tree.

When Aminayi was a fit man he loved looking at the sun set, collecting turtle eggs and watching the sparkling water flow with the ocean wind. He used to sit with baby Mia and rock her to sleep.

Aminayi used to love it when Maningawu baked him damper. He would wash it down with sweet black tea.

MIA starts thinking about going back to school. She misses footy training and singing with her friends. But there's a problem at home: Gloria has been caught driving without a licence and has to go to jail for six months.

No-one knows Glorianna's father. Gloria has never told anyone who he is, she's kept it a secret. Glorianna's dad is probably the wrong skin, a skin group Gloria is forbidden from marrying.

Maningawu is too old to look after baby Glorianna. She's scared she might fall asleep, and Glorianna might crawl off into the bush and get lost and something bad might happen to her.

Mia decides to stay at home and look after her little niece.

Mia is happy to live with Maningawu all the time and look after Glorianna, but she realises her future will disappear if she doesn't go back to school.

She sees her education, her footy competitions, her singing and all her dreams fading away like a rainbow after a storm. Most of all Mia wants to be a singer like Jessica Mauboy—who's coming to Tiwi Talent Time this year!

While Mia has been away from school, the magpie geese season has come and gone. Her friends and teammates miss her and wish she'd come back. The teachers, the principal and even the Tiwi liaison officer worry that Mia will fall too far behind to catch up on her work.

At a staff meeting they talk about how they can get Mia back to school. The school decides to give Mia and her grandma a house at the school, and set up daycare for baby Glorianna.

Mia is very happy to be back at school and works hard at everything. She gets back into the footy team and never misses training.

One day the girls fly to Darwin to play in the Quit 100 Cup competition. Jake decides to take on the responsibility of looking after baby

Glorianna for the very first time while Mia is away.

On the night of Tiwi Talent Time, Mia sings like a bird and Jessica Mauboy joins her on stage. Their song drives the audience wild. People stamp their feet, clap their hands and scream for more.

Mia can just see Maningawu through the spotlight, with Glorianna clapping and bouncing on her knee.

It feels good to be a star.

SKIN GROUPS

In Tiwi culture we have four different skin groups. You get your skin group (yiminga) from your mother and it lets you know who you can marry.

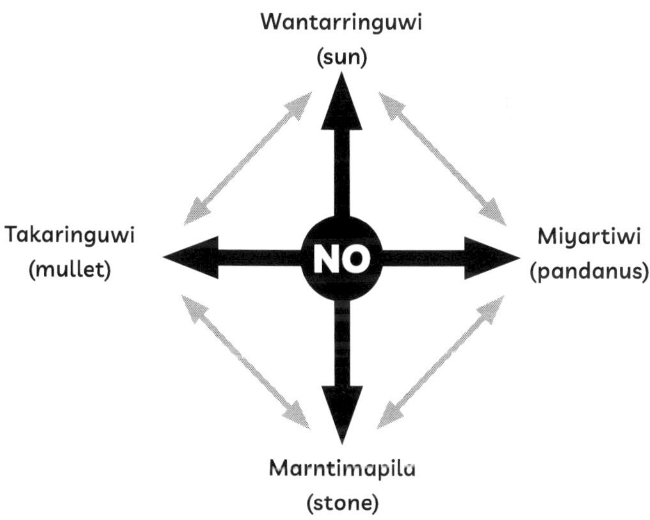

Skin groups are an important part of Tiwi culture. You can't marry someone from your own skin group or from the skin group directly opposite yours (in the diagram above).

For example, a person whose skin group is Marntimapila can't marry a person whose skin group is also Marntimapila or Wantarringuwi. Marntimapila can only marry people from the Takaringuwi and Miyartiwi skin groups.

MY HERO

Dear Adam Goodes,

You are my hero because you inspire me when you are on the field playing AFL. I also play football and my favourite position is centre and back line.

In the future I want to be a great role model like you. You are a good example to others of what it is to be a deadly strong Indigenous leader. I am proud of you for your campaign to stop racism in football and also for winning the Australian of the Year award. You stand for what's right for everyone. You are proud of your heritage and background, just like I am.

I've learnt to stand up for my rights by talking to different people and also looking after the young Tiwi children. You inspire me to work in a team and encourage my team mates.

I would like to wish you all the best for the future. Keep inspiring young people.

Bobette Joran

Dear Aminayi,

You're my hero, my role model, because you do everything for all of the Tiwi people. You are a good leader and you speak up for all the Tiwi people, for what we need and don't need, even with the government ministers in Canberra.

I'm proud that you – my grandfather – are the Chairman of the Tiwi Land Council for the Tiwi Islands.

You are a great person to look up to and you are always pushing us to keep going to school every day so that we don't miss a day. You want us to have a bright future and a good life, just like you did when you were young. You didn't give up hope and now you're a good role model for any young Tiwi person to look up to.

I'm grateful you taught me what's important in life: our people, our education, our culture.

Love,
Sharna Austral

Dear Jessica Mauboy,

You are my hero because you are the most beautiful, nicest woman I ever met. Maybe you remember that the senior Tiwi girls and I finally got to meet you yesterday for the first time.

When I saw you I couldn't stop looking at you; you were smiling all the time. We talked, laughed, and then we asked you to sing a song for us. Then we stood right there, watching you sing away. Your voice was so amazing, I couldn't stop listening. I was so happy to meet you. It's hard to believe it all happened.

I hope to see you again, especially because you are an Aboriginal, Indigenous person just like us. I can't wait to tell my family when we go back home all these wonderful stories about you.

xOx
Sherayne Puruntatameri

Hello, Andrew Gaff,

I look up to you, Gaff. You are my hero. I think you're a good footballer; you have the talent and you are a great midfielder. I like that you can kick with your opposite foot when you're going for goals and that you can run the field and make everyone believe that you're an awesome superstar.

I also play football like you and I've represented the Northern Territory Thunder Under-18s. I want to be a role model like you – a great leader and an amazing player. I want to play in the midfield and kick with the opposite foot and run around the field with a football in my arms, running rings around everyone. Watching you inspires me. I want to keep fit and play football like you and have a wonderful future.

Next season I will be going to New Zealand to play for the Woomeras Under-18s – that's a team for girls from remote communities. I feel so excited because it is a good opportunity and I'm making my family happy. I'm proud to be in a national squad competition. At home, back at

Tiwi, we play in a women's competition. We play for our school, Tiwi College, and we play against Garden Point, Milikapiti, and Wurrumiyanga. Last year I won best and fairest for the nine-a-side competition. My family was so excited for me and really proud.

Thanks for your inspiration, Gaff.

From,
Rina Moreen

Dear Dad,

You are my hero because you're a clever, supportive, loving person and also a teacher to me.

I see you, Dad, as a hero because when you were growing up you always treated everyone with respect and everyone respected you the same way, and you always put other people first.

I have learnt so much from you, like how you taught my brother, sister and me how to hunt and fish and go into bushes and mangroves to collect food whenever we are out camping or out for the day.

You are a teacher to me because you always encourage me to go to school and not miss a day, and you always talk to me about how education is important in life.

I would like to be like you because you are the person that I look up to as my hero. I'm so grateful to have you as part of my life; you are always there whenever I need you. You have always wanted me to achieve a higher level of education and become a good role model for the

Tiwi Islands and for our family.

Thank you for always supporting me and always encouraging me to have a good education.

Love always, your youngest daughter,
Jessica Therese Stassi

Dear Patty Mills,

I have chosen you as my hero because basketball is my passion. You have shown me everything about what you did to achieve your goals, to get to where you are now. I come from an Indigenous background and I know that you care a lot about your people and appreciate who you are.

It's amazing how you share your stories about your background and be proud of who you are. I admire what you do and how much of a role model you have become.

The things I have learnt from you are that you never give up and you always strive for excellence.

I want to achieve my goals in life, such as finishing school and graduating from Year 12 in 2017.

I attended an all-girls Catholic school in Canberra and played basketball games in Belconnen. For me, moving to Canberra from a remote community at Wurrumiyanga on Bathurst Island, which is part of Tiwi Islands, was a big step to finding and experiencing new things.

I wish to play basketball and, maybe one day

– if I work really hard just as you did – play in the WNBA. I look up to you because I want to make my people proud, to never give up, and to appreciate everything and everyone in my life. And make every moment count.

Whether I fail or succeed in what I do, I will always try my best as you did. You are my hero!

Thank you,
Angie Tipungwuti

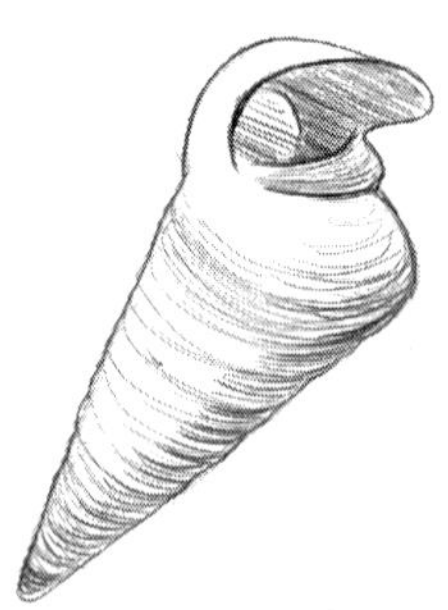

MY PROUDEST MOMENT

My proudest moment was being the first person from my family to leave Australia. Last year I had the opportunity to spend two weeks in Cambodia. I travelled with three of my classmates and my two teachers. There were other students and teachers from the Northern Territory and Victoria there too.

The weather was pretty hot and sticky, just like it is at home on the Tiwi Islands. Before we went to Cambodia we learnt some Khmer words that meant things like 'hello', 'my name is', 'thank you' and 'no thank you'. I also learnt a bit about the Cambodian culture and found out that we weren't allowed to wear singlets, T-shirts or shorts because our shoulders and knees needed to be covered.

I'm proud of working with some Cambodian children, helping them build a pathway and making a few things they needed for school. I also helped the monks build houses for those families who lost their houses during the war. The trip made me feel grateful for everything I have.

Bobette Joran

THE proudest moment of this year was when I applied and got a job at the local sports club. The first thing I had to do was learn how to write a résumé and cover letter. The résumé looked hard at first but when I did it, it was easy. The cover letter was a bit hard to do because it contained a lot of information.

The deputy principal helped me call the boss and discuss the job. I was nervous about handing my résumé to the boss. My maningawu helped me out by coming with me to hand in my résumé. My grandparents are always supporting and encouraging me.

I got the job and I'm really proud of myself for being motivated and going out and earning my own money.

I am feeling excited about the new job, meeting new people, learning new skills and saving money for the future.

Sharna Austral

My proudest moment was when the girls from Milikapiti, Wurrumiyanga and Garden Point went to Darwin on the ferry to play footy with the girls from there.

My teammates and I were selected to represent the Tiwi as a team, Together as One. We played with the Northern Territory Football League (NTFL) women and girls – the ones who played for the Waratahs and Tracy Village. That day I won the Best on Ground medal. My family were so proud of me and I was proud of myself, and very happy and excited.

When I got the medal, the two teams were lined up. The director of the Heart Foundation came to me and put the medal ribbon over my head. I felt scared because everyone was looking at me, but afterward I felt happy. Everyone clapped and cheered. I felt so happy that they were supporting me.

I was also proud last week when the teachers said that I might go to Sydney; if one of the other students didn't come to school the next week then I could take their place. The Principal, Smithy, and Ms Ailsa came to me and said, 'I'm so proud of you that you still come to school – you earned your chance to come to Sydney.' And I was proud of myself because I'd put the effort in to really try at school.

Sherayne Puruntatameri

One of my proudest moments was when I got four As in my maths exams. I had to work really hard to get my marks – a lot of homework and revision. If I got a question wrong I would have to go back and fix it up. Sometimes I would get stressed and confused and wouldn't do my work. After a while I started understanding more of my work with help from my teachers. Then the work became easier and more fun because I knew I was doing well.

When I thought I had done enough work for the day I would help my friend to do her booklet. I wouldn't tell her the answers but I would teach her so she could understand it a bit more. I would wait until my friend was up to me and then we would do the booklet together and help each other if needed.

Our classroom is very quiet when we work; all the girls have their heads down typing on their computers or writing. The girls in my class get a lot of work done; even when they have free time they just work and work.

I'm proud of myself and all the girls in my class because I know they are going to do a lot of amazing things when they are older. I know they will have great jobs and great responsibilities. They really do care about their work because they want a better future, and they are good role models for younger Tiwi kids.

Jasmine Brooks

MY HAPPIEST MOMENT

My houseparents Ms Nadine and Mr Dunstan were having their first child – my little brother – and I wasn't there to celebrate with them. They baked chocolate cake to celebrate the baby they were having. My big sister Dellarosa and some other girls from school were there, and Dellarosa cut the cake up.

Ms Nadine and Mr Dunstan went to Brisbane to give birth. My little brother Anaiah was born in spring, on 14 September 2014, and I couldn't wait to meet him.

I met my little brother after they came home from Brisbane. Ms Nadine came into the lounge room in our boarding house at Tiwi College and there he was: my cute little brother. He had black straight hair and beautiful brownish eyes. She gave him to me to hold. My little brother Anaiah was wrapped in a rug and had his eyes closed

He felt heavy and my arms started to shake. I felt happy, excited, nervous and filled with joy.

The next day I heard my little brother crying. I felt like a proud big sister to have him in my life. Having Anaiah as my little brother makes me feel more like a big sister in the family group home that my sister Dellarosa and I have lived in for almost four years now. Gup Gup was Anaiah's nickname given to him by family group home four.

Watching Anaiah grow from being a baby to a one-year-old makes me happy – he puts a smile on my face.

Shania Puruntatameri

THE happiest time of my life was travelling to New Zealand for the first time. I went on the trip with a bunch of Indigenous girls from all states in Australia. We were playing on an AFL team called the Woomeras. I was lucky to have my big sister Caitlyn to play alongside me. Our first flight was from Darwin to Melbourne and one of the Woomeras staff was waiting at Melbourne airport for us. We stayed in the hotel at the airport for a few hours until we headed to New Zealand. The rest of the team and our coaches and managers were already there waiting for us.

New Zealand was so cold that I had three jumpers on. Our team had to play the New Zealand Kahu, which is a Maori team. The New Zealanders are getting good at playing AFL and they're big and strong – they have hard tackles and hits. Our guernsey was red, black and yellow and the other team wore black and grey.

Seeing the New Zealand girls do the haka was amazing because they were telling us that they were ready to fight against us. We have a team song and the girls from each state sang something in their language to make the song even better. It took us a few days to get the song right.

And we won both of the games!

Ella Moreen

THE happiest day of my life was when I travelled to Europe with my father. We took a bus up from Canberra straight to the airport. The weather was nice and warm at night with a bit of rain. I remember wearing Timberland shoes, long blue jeans and a blue-sleeved shirt. I was listening to Jessica Mauboy, thinking about how much I was going to miss home.

The international airport in Sydney seemed crowded and noisy with the sound of footsteps, of people's shoes clanking on the marble tiles on the ground. As I walked towards my departure gate I felt anxious, nervous and excited, and I was trying to put a smile here and there to make people think I was happy.

My favourite moment was taking off. I was really excited that I was going to another place for the first time. I flew from Sydney to Bangkok, Bangkok to Dubai, Dubai to Madrid, and took a train from Madrid to Seville. I would take flights in and out of Spain and travel to places like Morocco, London, Scotland, Portugal, Italy, France and Abu Dhabi.

I really did enjoy going to Europe – my

favourite place was London. I loved the red buses and the black taxi cabs. I even got to walk across the Abbey Road crossing, just like The Beatles, and went to see Buckingham Palace.

Even though taking off for Europe was such a happy moment, I was just as happy when I came home to Wurrumiyanga, my community.

Angelita Tipungwuti

MY SACRED PLACE

THE place I like to go is Karslake over at Milikapiti, on Melville Island. Karslake is a famous Country of some Tiwi people. The Dutch went there over 300 years ago, long before Captain Cook. From Milikapiti it's just 15 minutes' drive to Karslake. As you drive you can see red rocky cliffs and calm smooth sea, and there are lots of palm trees.

It is the best camping place. I love going camping there because it's my grandfather's Country.

Beautiful place: strong wind, nice soft sand, you can see fish jumping up from the water. Walk on the beach and find seashells. When the tide is out you can hunt in the mangroves for mud mussels and long bums (a cone-shaped shell with a crunchy slug in it – it's like a snow cone but it's muddy). Cook your bush food on the fire and while it's cooking you can smell it. When it's cooked have a taste: it will be delicious.

If the tide is in you can go fishing or crack oysters on the rocks. If you want crabs you will need to walk the island with a spear. You can also go for a walk in the bush for wallaby.

I go camping there every year during the bush holiday. I also go hunting there with my family on weekends. When I'm there I feel comfortable because I'm used to that country.

Rina Moreen

My sacred place is Tiwi College because of my little brother Anaiah. I go to Tiwi College from Monday to Friday. When I get to Tiwi College I feel proud, happy and grateful. I see beautiful people come together as one big Picka family. I can see the perspiration on their faces, it looks like raindrops. I also love the beautiful smell of the bushes and flowers. I can smell the bush burning off. We burn off every year to clear the land. I can hear all the children on the basketball court shouting and playing hit the board, giggling and laughing.

I can touch the beautiful wet sand down at South Beach. Laying down on the sand I can feel the hard curved shells with hermit crabs sticking into my back with their claws. I taste the salty water and also the tasty chewy mud mussel.

Tiwi people find the mussels in the mud. They come in a shell that is curved like a cockle shell. When you cook it, the two sides of the shell open and the juice of the mud mussel is delicious. The juice of the soup when you are cooking a turtle on a fire or roasting dugong rib bones makes my guts rumble.

I see people going out hunting in the sea for dugong and turtle. You have to go on a boat to an island because the turtles like laying their eggs on sand. To catch dugong and turtle, you need a long stick from the bush and a bush harpoon. Fishing and hunting is a common modern Tiwi activity to do on a Sunday.

Shania Puruntatameri

My sacred place is Karslake, which is just out from Milikapiti. It is sacred to me because it's my grandmother's Country. During the bush holidays every year, I go out camping with my families. I even go to Karslake on the weekends for hunting or fishing, or to chill on the beach and enjoy the cool lovely breeze.

When we're at Karslake we can see the iron houses that people have made. Every morning after breakfast my siblings, nieces, nephews and I go down to the beach and my brothers use a throwing net to catch mullets to use as bait.

When we're driving out to the bush we can smell the bushfire that the rangers light for the burn-off. When the tide is out we can hunt for mud mussels, long bums, mangrove worms, oysters and mud crabs. When the tide is high we can fish; the men go out and hunt for turtles and dugong on the boat.

At night people love to go out possum hunting, shooting for wallaby and buffalo or looking for carpet snakes on the road or in logs. Karslake is a nice and peaceful place to be but my grandmother says that the old people who were buried there don't like loud noises. The old people also don't like it when kids dig holes in the ground. If you dig holes, you will get punished and there will be strong winds or you won't get food.

Ella Moreen

MY sacred place I like to go to is Karslake. I only go there a couple of times a year when my family goes camping. The place is sacred to me because I feel safe with my ancestors and my family and it also makes me feel free. It's a place where everyone loves me.

When I'm there I can see the lovely beach with beautiful white sand, nice cool trees and Pukumani poles (cemetery poles). When I'm there alone I like to sit on a log and watch the sun go down and see the beautiful colourful sky.

I can smell the fresh new plants and the salty air from the sea, and the mud mussels cooking on the fire.

When I lie near the campfire I can hear a lot of animals at night, like birds, dingos, bandicoots and possums; I can also hear other people in the camps laughing and having a good time.

When I'm at Karslake I can touch and feel the soft white sands that I like to build castles out of. I can also touch the cool, smooth sea that smells like salt. I feel the rough surface of the pine trees that I like to sit under. When night comes I can feel the fire making me warm when I'm feeling cold.

There are some rules: if people are drunk and making noise they have to be quiet, because the old people who are buried there don't like it and they can get really mad.

Jasmine Brooks

My sacred place is Ten Mile Beach, which is located on the Tiwi Islands. It's a wonderful place to relax and enjoy the breeze and swim in the cool see-through water. I go there when it's bush holidays in June/July, when the grass is brown and the sky is blue. I also go out there on weekends to fish and hunt for mud mussels, long bums (a cone-shaped shell with a slug inside), mud crabs, oysters, mangrove worms, and stingrays.

I feel like I'm in heaven when I sit by the beach, listening to birds and the sound of the waves crashing onto the sandbanks. When I'm on the beach I can see birds flying, sand crabs crawling around, long tom fish skipping on the water, and children playing and laughing.

I smell salty water, fresh fish cooking and mussels sizzling on the hot ash. I hear kids laughing and playing on the beach, birds singing in my ear, wind whistling through the trees and tea boiling. I can touch the hard shell of a big mud crab, the scales of a fish, lumpy sticks and dry leaves.

I can taste salt water and salty sand.

I go out to Ten Mile Beach with my family to share our love and remember our family that have passed on, and to show people that we love that place and we will cherish that place for generations.

Jess Stassi

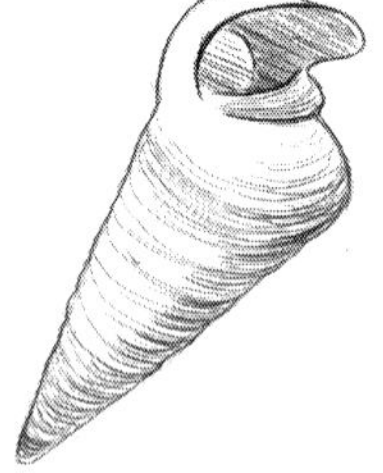

GLOSSARY

alalinguwi jarrakarlinga young girl or teenage girl

aminayi Tiwi word for grandpa (a mother's father or father's father)

arlaminga barramundi

awungana hello

barra short for barramundi

basic card Centrelink BasicsCard used for buying food and clothing

bush holidays June/July school holidays: Tiwi people go camping/hunting in various locations on the islands

bush tucker food from the bush such as native plums and apples, wallaby and buffalo

community small town with a shop, school, clinic and childcare centre

Cyril Rioli Australian Football League player from the Tiwi Islands (played with Hawthorn Football Club)

family group home house where up to 12 students live at boarding school

Garden Point community of Melville Island, also known as Pularumpi or Pirlangimpi

growled/growling getting in trouble

hit the board a modified game of AFL football played on a basketball court

houseparent someone who looks after you at boarding school

Japparika team song for the Tiwi Bombers

jarranga buffalo

Jessica Mauboy Aboriginal singer, songwriter and actor from Darwin

jipwajirringa wallaby

jukwarringa mud mussel, shellfish (like a clam) found in mangroves

karluwu no

kirimpika mud crab, dark green-black crab found in mangroves or beaches

kuwa yes

long bum edible sea snail in a cone-shaped shell

maningawu grandmother, mother's mother

Menindee small regional town in far west New South Wales

Milikapiti community on Melville Island, also known as Snake Bay Community

miputi fish

mission place once run by the Catholic Church that was once used to house Aboriginal children and teach them White ways

nginingawila our

ngirramini story

nimpangi goodbye

NTFL/AFLNT Northern Territory Australian Football League

outstation campsite out in the bush, a long way from amenities and towns

pamantarri damper, doughy bread cooked on hot ashes on a campfire or in an oven

pay week when the government makes welfare payments to parents and carers

Quit 100 Cup Northern Territory Australian Football League competition held in Darwin for secondary school-age girls

skin group kinship system that determines marriage lines (see also page 29)

Stolen Generations Aboriginal children, once termed 'half-caste', who were taken away from their families and put into missions

tiyari magpie geese season, end of the dry season and beginning of the wet, known as the build-up season, when young geese grow into adults

troopy troop carrier, a large four-wheel drive that carries up to 10 passengers

turnumuni salmon

upstairs house house built on stilts

Wurrimiyanga largest community on the Tiwi Islands

yiminga skin group

yurwuli mangrove worm, found in logs in mangroves

ACKNOWLEDGEMENTS

The two books brought together in this edition were made possible with support from Alison Lester, Dr Anita Heiss, Pamela Freeman, Wendy Rapee, Nicky Shortridge, HarperCollins Publishers Australia, Hachette Australia, Tiwi College teachers Dianne (Tictac) Moore, Bronny Burger and Ebony Humbert, and, of course, the talented Senior Girls class.

Sincere thanks also to the Norman Family Bequest, given in memory of Hachette publisher Matt Richell, for their sponsorship of *Nginingawila Ngirramini: Our Story*.

ABOUT THE AUTHORS

Tiwi Girl

Tiwi College students Dellarosa Puruntatameri, Edwina Mungatopi, Juliette Puruntatameri, Jessica Stassi, Gabriella Lorenzo, Bobette Minniecon, Caitlyn Moreen, Elenora Moreen and Alexandra Guy in wrote the original version of *Tiwi Girl*, with guidance from mentor Alison Lester and assistant teacher Dianne (Tictac) Moore.

A longer version of the story, featured in this book, was created by the whole Senior Girls class – Alexandra Guy, Angelita Tipungwuti, Arthurina Moreen, Bobette Minniecon, Caitlyn Moreen, Dellarosa Puruntatameri, Edwina Mungatopi, Elenora Moreen, Gabriella Lorenzo, Jasmine Brooks, Jessica Stassi, Juliette Puruntatameri, Kathleen Puruntatameri, Kimberley Cunningham, Shania Puruntatameri and Sharna Austral – supported by Alison, Tictac and teacher Ebonie Humbert.

Nginingawila Ngirramini: Our Story

The Sydney workshop for this book included Angelita Tipungwuti, Bobette Joran, Ella Moreen, Jasmine Brooks, Jess Stassi, Rina Moreen, Shania Puruntatameri, Sharna Austral and Sheryane Puruntatameri. They were supported by workshop leader Dr Anita Heiss and mentor Pamela Freeman, as well as teachers Ebonie Humbert and Dianne 'Tictac' Moore.

ABOUT TIWI COLLEGE

Tiwi College is located at Pickertaramoor on Melville Island. The secondary college is a weekly boarding facility where students are accommodated in family group homes. It caters for holistic learning, helping young Tiwi people become ready for work.

The college is owned and managed by the Tiwi people through the Tiwi Education Board, comprising senior men and women from all Tiwi communities.

The Tiwi Islands are made up of two islands, Melville and Bathurst, and four communities. But we are all one people, Tiwi.

ABOUT THE INDIGENOUS LITERACY FOUNDATION

The Indigenous Literacy Foundation (ILF) is a national charity working with Aboriginal and Torres Strait Islander remote Communities across Australia. We are Community-led, responding to requests from remote Communities for culturally relevant books, including early learning board books, resources, and programs to support Communities to create and publish their stories in languages of their choice.

In 2024 the ILF won the Astrid Lindgren Memorial Award, given annually to a person or organisation for their outstanding contribution to children's or young adult literature.

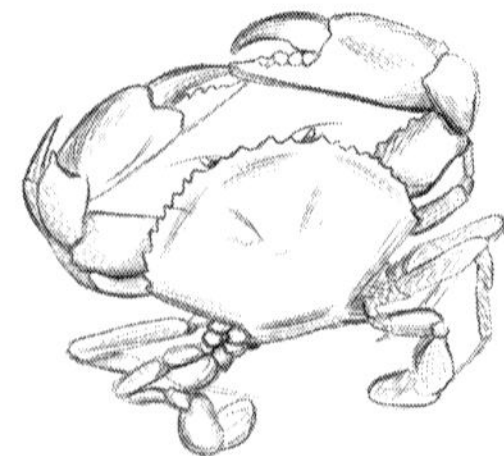